My Friend Max
A Story About A Friend With Autism

By Reena B. Patel, MA, LEP, BCBA

Illustrated by Rashi Saxena

KIND EYE PUBLISHING, LLC

ISBN-13: 978-0999226230 Kind Eye Publishing, LLC

ISBN-10: 0999226231

I dedicate this book

To all children who have felt different or felt they do not belong.

To my parents and sisters for their endless support and love.

To my husband Bijal, who is the strongest and most compassionate person I know.

To my children, Ayana, Maliya, and Jivaan who inspire me every day and remind us to see the good in everything.

To my MARS friends who have never left my side.

Hello! My name is Ayana and I attend Willow Elementary School. So does my friend, Max. Max has Autism. This means Max's brain understands the things we see, smell, hear, taste, and touch differently. This makes it difficult for Max to talk, listen, understand, play, and learn. But, it doesn't mean he can't do it.

Even though Max has Autism, we are a lot alike.

We both like to sing songs, do puzzles, and play on the swings.

Aa Bb Cc Dd Ee Ff Gg Hh Ii J

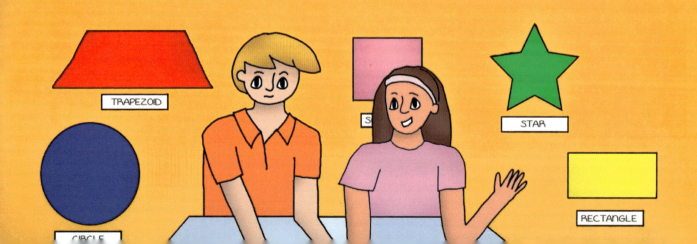

I am very lucky! Ms. Vicki chose me to be Max's special buddy to help him in class. It's hard for him to talk to people, to make new friends and to follow directions. I feel happy when I help Max.

Every Monday before school, Max and his mom wait for me by the school office. Then, we walk together to Ms. Vicki's class to start our day.

First, I help Max put his backpack away when he comes to class. Ms. Vicki says having Max's name and picture by his cubby helps him remember where to put it. She's right. He's really good at that.

Next, when Ms. Vicki rings the bell, we sit on special spots on the floor for morning circle time. Every day I look for my red star, and Max looks for his blue star. Having the same color each time helps guide Max where to go. Ms. Vicki calls it a *visual*.

Today, Ms. Vicki is letting each of us pick a song to sing as a group. It's my turn when the "Magic Wand" is passed to me. I choose *"The Wheels on the Bus."* After we sing my song, I pass the wand to Max. He is supposed to keep his wand and hands in his lap, but Max begins to move it around in circles. Ms. Vicki shows Max a picture of a child with hands in their lap. Max looks at it, and remembers to do the same.

Max has trouble picking a song for us to sing. I know his favorite song is *"If You're Happy and You Know It."* I whisper the first few words to Max. He smiles and begins to sing the song. We all join in. The whole class enjoys singing that song. Ms. Vicki thanks me for being such a good helper.

After songs, Ms. Vicki claps her hands three times. That is our signal to move on to our next activity. There is a schedule with pictures on it for Max at our table.

Max sees on his schedule that we have "art" next. We walk to the art table and he places the "art" picture from his schedule in a paper pocket. For our art project, Max and I glue colored tissue squares on paper to make a special design. I help Max. The other friends in our class see us work as a team.

STUDENT'S ARTWORK

After art, it is recess time! Max and I love to swing. Ms. Vicki explains to me that Max likes the feeling of moving back and forth. Max has a hard time waiting his turn, but we each count out loud to 25, "1, 2, 3, 4..." to help us know whose turn is next.

When the bell rings, it is time to leave the playground and go back to class. Max follows me to our line and we walk into our classroom.

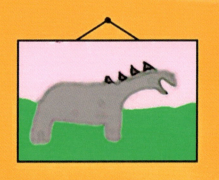

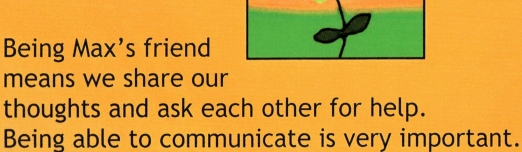

Being Max's friend means we share our thoughts and ask each other for help. Being able to communicate is very important.

When I speak to Max he may have trouble understanding some words I say. Ms. Vicki says his brain might have a hard time taking in so many words at one time. When I speak to Max, I use simple sentences. Sometimes, we match pictures to our words.

At the end of the day, we line up on a star on the floor by the door. One by one, Ms. Vicki taps our shoulder with a smile and tells us to get our backpack from our cubby and then to return to line.

Max is good about coming back to line. Max and I get excited that it's time to go home!

Before we leave, Ms. Vicki reminds us how special each of us are in our own ways. She says, "Friends help one another. Friends play together, share together, and laugh together."

Ms. Vicki reaches out her hand. One by one we give her a high five.

Then, we go to our parents. Max's mom is standing right next to my dad and they both give us a big hug before taking us home.

Max is my very best friend. I know I'm his friend, too.

People with Autism can learn a lot from us, and we can learn a lot from them, too. We can learn to better understand that we are similar in certain ways. We can learn to accept people who have differences. We can also learn to have positive attitudes toward people who may be different from us.

The ability to help someone is a gift we must cherish. While each of us is different in some ways, we can still be friends. "Friends who learn together, learn to live together."

HOW TO BE A FRIEND TO SOMEONE WITH AUTISM:

- *Many people with Autism are smart, but just in a different way. Try to find out what is the best way to interact with him or her.*

- *Never be afraid to ask your teacher questions about the students in your class who have Autism.*

- *Be accepting of the differences that they may have.*

- *When you communicate with your friend who has Autism, make sure to speak in simple sentences. You may even use gestures, like pointing when you talk.*

- *Use pictures as a visual and write or draw out what you want to say to help your friend understand.*

- *Try to include your friend in games by asking him or her to join in. Teach him or her how to play the game by showing them what to do.*

- *Participate in activities that interests your friend.*

- *Be flexible and patient by allowing your friend extra time to answer your questions.*

- *Try to sit close to your friend when possible and help do things if they need your help.*

- *Share the knowledge and understanding you have about Autism by teaching other kids about it.*

About the Author

Reena B. Patel, MA, LEP, BCBA, has had the privilege of working with families and children supporting all aspects of education and positive wellness for the past two decades as a Guidance Counselor, Licensed Educational Psychologist, and Board Certified Behavior Analyst. Ms. Patel has worked extensively with typically developing children as well as with children with exceptional needs, supporting their academic, behavioral and social development. She routinely holds workshops throughout California, guiding and training parents and educators on the purpose of inclusion and how it can be beneficial for all children.

Ms. Patel lives in San Diego, California with her husband and three children.
She reminds us to "be grateful, be present, be you".

For more information regarding the author and her practice AutiZm & More, please visit www.autizmandmore.com.